T0080637

Goods

HEINLE CENGAGE Learning™

Y|S|G A YBM COMPANY Young & Son Global, Inc.

What do you buy at the market?

Contents

Vocabulary	4
What Are Goods?	6
Things People Grow	8
Things People Make	10
Goods	12
Summary	14
Song	15
Index	16

Vocabulary
grow
farm
make

factory
buy
sell

Goods are everywhere.
We use goods every day.

People use computers.

People use paper and pencils.

People eat fruit.

People drink milk.

What are goods?

Where does corn come from?
First, a farmer grows corn on a farm.
Next, the farmer sends the corn
to a market.
Then, we buy the corn.
Things that farmers grow are goods.

1 Growing
2 Sending
3 Buying

Where does a bicycle come from?
First, a worker makes a bicycle
in a factory.
Next, the factory sends the bicycle
to a store.
Then, we buy the bicycle.
Things that workers make are goods.

1 Making
2 Sending
3 Buying

Fruits are goods.
Toys are goods, too.

She sells clothes at the store.

He sells food at the market.

Goods are things that people grow or make to sell.

Summary

How do these become goods?

corn

bicycle

Song

Goods! Goods!

Goods! Goods! Goods! Goods!
We grow goods. We make goods.
We sell goods. We buy goods.
We all use goods every day!

Goods! Goods! Goods! Goods!
We grow goods. We make goods.
We sell goods. We buy goods.
We all use goods every day!

Index

bicycle, 10

buy, 8–11

corn, 8

factory, 10

farm, 8

fruit, 7, 12

goods, 6–8, 10, 12–13

grows, 8–9, 13

makes, 10–11, 13

market, 8, 13

sells, 13

sends, 8–11

store, 10, 13

toys, 12

use, 6